MAE JEMISON

BY JANEY LEVY

Gareth Stevens
PUBLISHING

Please visit our website, www.garethstevens.com. For a free color catalog of all our high-quality books, call toll free 1-800-542-2595 or fax 1-877-542-2596.

Cataloging-in-Publication Data

Names: Levy, Janey.
Title: Mae Jemison / Janey Levy.
Description: New York : Gareth Stevens Publishing, 2019. | Series: Heroes of black history | Includes glossary and index.
Identifiers: ISBN 9781538231326 (pbk.) | ISBN 9781538230206 (library bound) | ISBN 9781538233122 (6 pack)
Subjects: LCSH: Mae, Mae, 1956–Juvenile literature. | African American women astronauts–Biography–Juvenile literature.
| Astronauts–United States–Biography–Juvenile literature.
Classification: LCC TL789.85.J46 L48 2019 | DDC 629.450092 B–dc23

First Edition

Published in 2019 by
Gareth Stevens Publishing
111 East 14th Street, Suite 349
New York, NY 10003

Copyright © 2019 Gareth Stevens Publishing

Designer: Katelyn E. Reynolds
Editor: Joshua Turner

Photo credits: Cover, p. 1 (Mae Jemison) Afro American Newspapers/Gado/Getty Images; cover, pp. 1–32
(background image) NASA/Tony Gray and Tom Farrar; p. 5 (main) NASA/BotMultichillT/Wikipedia.org; p. 5 (inset)
NASA/Adam Cuerden/Wikipedia.org; pp. 7, 27 Brendan Hoffman/Getty Images; p. 9 (stars) Triff/Shutterstock.com;
p. 9 (planets) Vadim Sadovski/Shutterstock.com; p. 9 (fish) aastock/Shutterstock.com; p. 9 (ocena) Dmitry Polonskiy/
Shutterstock.com; p. 9 (rock) Miroslav Orincak/Shutterstock.com; p 9 (lightening) swa182/Shutterstock.com; p. 9 (worm)
Palmi Gudmundsson/Shutterstock.com; p. 9 (pus) Dch-Kang/Shutterstock.com; pp. 11, 15 Bettmann/Getty Images;
p. 13 Godong/UIG via Getty Images; pp. 17, 19, 21, 29 courtesy of NASA; p. 23 Ron Galella, Ltd./WireImage/Getty
Images; p. 25 China Photos/Getty Images.

Printed in the United States of America

CPSIA compliance information: Batch #CW19GS: For further information contact Gareth Stevens, New York, New York at 1-800-542-2595.

CONTENTS

Words in the glossary appear in **bold** type the first time they are used in the text.

MAE JEMISON, ASTRONAUT EXTRAORDINAIRE

From the time Mae Jemison was very young, she dreamed of being a scientist and an astronaut. She was fortunate to have a family that supported and encouraged her dreams.

Mae was accepted by NASA (National **Aeronautics** and Space Administration) for astronaut training in 1987. In 1992, she became the first African American woman in space when she served as the science **mission** specialist on the space shuttle *Endeavour*. On the way to that historic accomplishment, she had already become a doctor, an engineer, and a **volunteer** in the **Peace Corps**. Mae has lived a truly extraordinary life.

MAE ON HER DREAMS

Mae said, "I always assumed [thought] I would go into space. Not necessarily as an astronaut; I thought because we were on the moon when I was 11 or 12 years old, that we would be going to Mars—I'd be going to work on Mars as a scientist."

Sally Ride

Mae was inspired to follow her astronaut dream by the historic flight of Sally Ride, the first American woman in space.

GROWING UP CURIOUS

Mae Jemison was born in Decatur, Alabama, on October 17, 1956. Her family moved to Chicago, Illinois, when she was 3 years old, and that's where she grew up. Mae was the youngest of three children in her family. Her father was a **maintenance** worker and carpenter, and her mother was a teacher.

A YOUNG SCIENTIST'S EXPERIMENT

Scientists learn about the world by carrying out experiments and young Mae was no exception. An **infection** she had as a child inspired her to carry out an extended experiment on pus. Pus is the thick, yellowish-white, liquid matter the body forms in response to an infection. Yuck!

Mae's interest in science began at a young age. When talking about science, she once said, "I was excited about the world around me. . .[I] think . . . it was the creativity that drew me to [science]. The possibilities. Understanding what was going on in the world around me."

Mae's childhood interest in science became a lifelong love, and she works to inspire young people today.

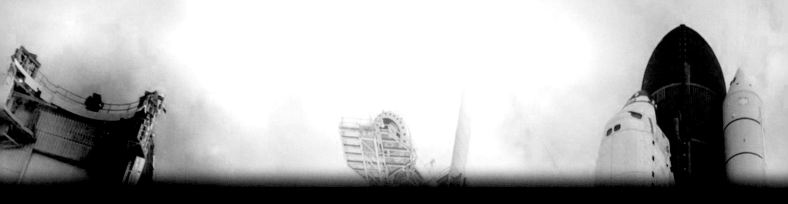

Mae has told many stories about how her childhood encouraged and inspired her love of science. She has described her family's summer fishing trips, where she loved playing with the worms and fish and learning all about them.

Mae has also talked about how she would look up at the stars with her uncle, and he would tell her they were really suns, just like our sun. They only looked small because they were so very far away. He even talked to her about very advanced ideas in the scientific field of **physics**, ideas people usually only study when they get to college.

"I WANT TO BE A SCIENTIST"

When Mae was very young, a teacher asked what she wanted to be. She said, "I want to be a scientist." The teacher thought the only thing a little girl could be that had to do with science was a nurse, so she said, "Don't you mean a nurse?" But Mae was firm. She said, "No, I mean a scientist."

THE MANY SIDES OF SCIENCE

SCIENCE

Science covers many subjects, from the study of worms and pus to the study of stars and space. Mae was interested in all of it!

AN IMPRESSIVE EDUCATION

By the time Mae was just 16, she had graduated from high school and started college. She attended Stanford University in California on a **scholarship**. She graduated from Stanford in 1977 with a **degree** in chemical engineering. While completing this challenging degree, she had also managed to fulfill all the requirements for a degree in African American studies.

Mae went to medical school at Cornell University in New York. After graduating in 1981, she had an internship at the Los Angeles County–University of Southern California Medical Center. An internship is a year in which a young doctor finishes his or her medical education by working in a hospital.

THERE'S MORE

Mae's degrees aren't her only remarkable educational accomplishments. While she was in medical school, she took dance classes at the famous Alvin Alley American Dance Theater in New York City. She also speaks three languages in addition to English: Russian, Japanese, and Swahili!

Here is Mae as an intern in her office at the Los Angeles County–University of Southern California Medical Center.

EARLY CAREER

After Mae finished her internship, she volunteered with the Peace Corps in Africa. She served as a medical officer for Liberia and Sierra Leone from 1983 to 1985.

Mae had a number responsibilities in her Peace Corps job. She was in charge of the system for supplying health care for the Peace Corps staff. She managed laboratory and medical staff. She taught personal health training for volunteers. She created health and safety guidelines. She also worked with the National Institutes of Health and the Centers for Disease Control on **research** projects for vaccines.

"NEVER BE LIMITED"

Sometimes it seems as if Mae accomplished more than one person possibly could. How did she do it? Here's something she said about how she approached life: "Never be limited by other people's limited imaginations. . . . If you adopt their attitudes, then the possibility won't exist because you'll have already shut it out."

The Peace Corps continues to carry out projects in African nations ranging from health care to education and more.

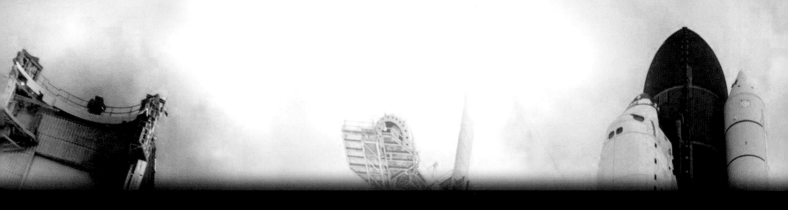

Mae returned to the United States in 1985 and took a job as a doctor with CIGNA Health Plans of California. But, as was usual for her, that wasn't all she did. She also took graduate-level engineering classes in Los Angeles and applied for admission to NASA's astronaut program.

Mae had always believed she would go into space, even though all astronauts were white men while she was growing up. In 1983, Sally Ride became the first American woman to go into space. Mae felt that Ride's flight meant more opportunities had opened up at NASA, so she applied. And a new part of her life began.

"WHAT WOULD ALIENS THINK OF HUMANS?"

Mae said that, even as a child, she thought the fact that all astronauts were white men and there was not a single woman was "one of the dumbest things in the world." She said she worried what aliens, or people from other worlds, would think about humans. She wondered if they would think that men were the only humans.

A happy Mae appears here after being accepted into the astronaut program.

LIFE AT NASA

In 1987, Mae was accepted as an astronaut candidate. More than 2,000 people had applied, but only 15—including Mae—were selected! Then the training began.

The astronaut candidates had to learn the basics of the **space shuttle**. They also had to learn how to work as part of a team, just as they would do in space. In addition, they took classes. The classes covered science, medical procedures, public speaking, and survival training. Candidates got a feel for what they would be doing in space by practicing on a life-sized model of the space shuttle.

PREPARING FOR SPACE WALKS

Sometimes in space, astronauts have to go outside their spaceship to work. These events are called space walks. To learn how to move and work during space walks, astronaut candidates go underwater in an enormous swimming pool. They float in the water while they practice on life-sized models of spaceships. These practice periods may last up to 7 hours!

Astronaut candidates have the opportunity to experience brief periods of weightlessness, since in space they will be floating weightlessly all of the time.

Mae completed her astronaut training in 1988. But she didn't go into space right away. She had other jobs at NASA first. Mae worked on launch, or send-off, support activities at the Kennedy Space Center in Florida. She also tested the exactness of shuttle computer software. In addition, she worked on different science support group activities.

Finally, in 1992, Mae accomplished her dream of going to the stars. She became the science mission specialist for mission STS-47 Spacelab-J on the space shuttle *Endeavour*. This mission launched from Kennedy Space Center on September 12, 1992, and returned there on September 20, 1992.

WHAT'S A SCIENCE MISSION SPECIALIST?

Some astronauts are pilots, which means they fly the spacecraft. Others are called mission specialists. They may be engineers, scientists, or doctors, and they have special skills related to the flight's particular mission. Mae's background in both engineering and medicine made her a perfect choice to be a science mission specialist.

Mae and her fellow astronauts are walking to the shuttle on the day of the launch.

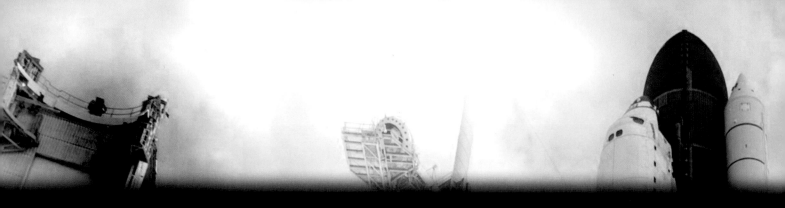

The United States and Japan worked together on mission STS-47 Spacelab-J. Mae was in space for 190 hours, 30 minutes, 23 seconds—almost 8 days. During those 8 days, the shuttle flew around Earth 127 times! Mae spent much of her time inside the shuttle's Spacelab, carrying out experiments. Altogether, 44 experiments were carried out. Some experiments were in life sciences, and some were in material sciences, which have to do with creating new kinds of matter for particular purposes. Mae also played an important part in the mission's bone cell research experiment.

This was Mae's only space mission. She left NASA in March 1993.

SPACELAB

The Spacelab used on Mae's mission was created by the European Space Agency and was meant to be used for research on space missions. It was set up inside a large area inside the shuttle. It held everything needed for the research, including computers, work stations, supplies, tools, and materials to conduct experiments.

Mae appears here inside
the Spacelab on *Endeavour.*

21

AWARDS AND HONORS

By the time Mae left NASA, she had collected a large number of honors and awards in recognition of her many accomplishments. She was honored by *Essence* magazine in 1988. In 1989, she was named Gamma Sigma Gamma Woman of the Year, and later made the list of *McCall's* magazine's 10 Outstanding Women for the '90s in 1991.

Mae was awarded Johnson Publications Black Achievement Trailblazers Award in 1992, the same year she went into space. Also in 1992, Wright Junior College in Chicago opened the Mae C. Jemison Science and Space Museum, which was named in her honor.

MORE HONORS

In 1993, the year Mae left NASA, *Ebony* magazine named her to its Most Influential Women list. She was also admitted to the National Women's Hall of Fame that same year. Mae is also a member of the National Medical Association Hall of Fame and the Texas Science Hall of Fame.

Even though she left NASA in 1993, Mae has remained an influential woman and scientist.

LIFE AFTER NASA

Mae didn't retire after leaving NASA. In March 1993—the same month she left NASA—she founded her own company, the Jemison Group, Inc. Her company creates projects meant to help people in the developing world. The term "developing world" indicates countries that have fewer economic and **technological** advantages. The Jemison Group's projects have worked to improve health in western Africa and ways to make electricity for developing countries.

Mae also wants to encourage a love of science among young people. In 1994, she founded the Earth We Share. This is an international science camp for students aged 12 to 16.

A REAL ASTRONAUT PLAYS AN ASTRONAUT

As a child, Mae was a fan of the television series *Star Trek*. Actor LeVar Burton—who played Geordi La Forge on *Star Trek: The Next Generation*—learned that and asked Mae if she would like to be on the series. And, in 1993, she wound up playing Lieutenant Palmer in an episode.

Mae is a highly sought after speaker, giving speeches at schools, businesses, and public events.

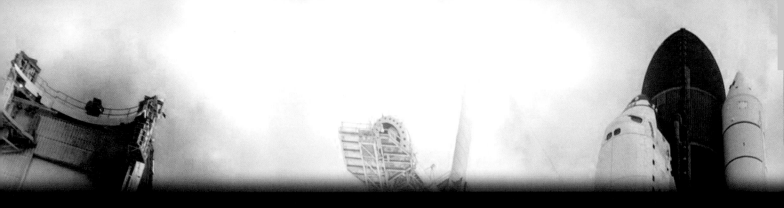

Of course, running her own company and an international science camp weren't enough for Mae. In 1995, she began teaching **environmental** studies at Dartmouth College in New Hampshire. She taught there until 2002.

Although Mae is no longer at Dartmouth, she still teaches because she believes in the importance of education. She has said, "I want to make sure we use all our talent, not just 25 percent. Don't let anyone rob you of your imagination, your creativity, or your curiosity. It's your place in the world; it's your life." She currently has a teaching position at Cornell University in New York.

MAE AT HOME

Mae isn't all work and no play. She loves animals and has two cats to keep her company, while she also engages in numerous hobbies like photography, skiing, and dance. Mae also studies a number of other languages, which is important when you are truly a global figure.

Mae often speaks to students, helping to inspire the next generation with her own story.

27

KEEP REACHING FOR THE STARS

Today, Mae hasn't slowed down. If anything, she's busier than ever. In addition to the Jemison Group, she runs a business called BioSentient Corporation. It's a medical device company that creates devices people can wear. The devices track how a person's body is acting in different situations and train them in how to deal with situations that cause anxiety and worry.

Mae is also leading a project called 100 Year Starship. Its goal is to make sure we're ready to send humans to a star beyond our solar system within the next 100 years. What a remarkable woman!

MAE THE WRITER

Mae has also written several books. *Find Where the Wind Goes: Moments from My Life* is a book about her life. Several of her books have been for children. They include: *The 100 Year Starship, Journey Through Our Solar System, Discovering New Planets,* and *Exploring Our Sun.*

MAE JEMISON'S ACCOMPLISHMENTS

CHEMICAL ENGINEER

DOCTOR

PEACE CORPS VOLUNTEER

NASA ASTRONAUT

FOUNDER OF THE JEMISON GROUP

FOUNDER OF THE EARTH WE SHARE

ACTOR

TEACHER

WRITER

PUBLIC SPEAKER

FOUNDER OF BIOSENTIENT CORPORATION

HEAD OF 100 YEAR STARSHIP

Mae's accomplishments are truly amazing!

GLOSSARY

aeronautics: the science that deals with the operation of aircraft

degree: a title given to students by a college or university after having successfully completed a course of study

environmental: having to do with the conditions that surround a living thing and affect the way it lives

infection: the spread of germs inside the body, causing illness

maintenance: having to do with the labor of keeping something in a state of repair

mission: a task or job a group must perform

Peace Corps: a government agency that encourages world peace and friendship by having American volunteers provide skilled help in countries around the world

physics: the study of matter, energy, force, and motion, and the relationship among them

research: studying to find something new

scholarship: money awarded to a student to pay for his or her college education

space shuttle: a NASA spacecraft that could be used more than once

technological: having to do with the practical application of specialized knowledge

volunteer: a person who works without being paid

FOR MORE INFORMATION

BOOKS

Barghoorn, Linda. *Mae Jemison: Trailblazing Astronaut, Doctor, and Teacher.* New York: Crabtree Publishing, 2017.

Dong, Monique. *Mae Jemison.* New York: Simon Spotlight, 2016.

Lassieur, Allison. *Astronaut Mae Jemison.* Minneapolis, MN: Lerner Publications, 2017.

WEBSITES

Dr. Mae Jemison
jemisonfoundation.org/about/mae-jemison
Read about what Mae has been doing since she left NASA.

Mae Jemison Biography
www.notablebiographies.com/Ho-Jo/Jemison-Mae.html
Learn more about Mae's life.

INDEX